Prison Segmentation For Security

Reverend Mike Wanner

Copyright

August 11, 2017

Reverend Mike Wanner

Selected Images Used by License

Table Of Contents

Introduction 4
1 - I am Writing This Book Because 5
2 - The Intensity of Space Density 9
3 - Space Segmentation 10
4 - Space & Security Reactivity 11
5 - Space Can Help Reduce Stress 13
6 - How Can Space Be Used Differently? 14
7 - Initial Analysis 15
8 - Space Use Security Goals 16
9 - Essential Service In the Segments 17
10 - How Would Security Segmentation Work? 18
11 - Segmentation Could Decrease Density 19
12 - Segmentation Can Be Foundational 20
13 - Space Reorganizational Ideas 21
14 - Redesign Teams 23
15 - Future Prison Segment Sizes - Whichever Works Best ... 25
16 - Rehabilitation 26
17 - Universal Prayer For Prisons 27
18 - Thank You 28
19 - Don't Worry Ever 29
21 - Angels Please Prayers 32
22 - Private Channeling 33
23 - Reverend Mike Wanner 34

Introduction

In America alone, there are about 2.3 million people in 6,000+ jails or prisons.

All those prisoners have unique challenges and opportunities which can create challenges to their peace and security. The problems of one prisoner can contribute to situations that could have a domino effect on others under certain circumstances.

I, like most people, was oblivious to that fact until I was invited to look into it. I started channeling Angel Raphael in 2013 and began releasing little message sets as they came through.

In message set 16 of the Angel Raphael Speaks Series there was a message that has remained floating in my head since as a topic for my writing.

"I asked Mike to Step into Prison Energetically

I have asked Mike to get the address and location within a prison of a designated space so he can visit energetically and receive feedback for us. Whether he will have time, interest or opportunity to do this will be interesting to see. As he writes this, he is not thrilled with the idea. We are already consuming a lot of his time." ARS16

After the First Three Hundred messages, I published Three Angel Raphael Speaks Volumes and much more on healing but the topic of prisons is very complicated so there was a delay.

1 - I am Writing This Book Because

I embraced the invitation in 2016. So far, The Angel Raphael prodding has had me publish the following books related to prisons:

1. *Angel Raphael Speaks Volume 4: Angels, Addicts, Alcoholics & Prisoners - Oh Yeah!*
2. *Angel Raphael Speaks Volume 5: Prisoners Caring for Alcoholics - Australia In Miniature   Projects Intro*
3. *Angel Raphael Speaks Volume 6: Prisoners Caring for Addicts - Australia In Miniature For   Addicts*
4. *Prison Jobs Now: Providing Care For Addicts And Alcoholics*
5. *Angel Raphael Speaks - Prisons (A Kindle only book -2013)*
6. *Contained Care Communities: Concept*
7. *Australia In Miniature*
8. *Prison Possibilities Dialogue Series: Concept*
9. *Prison Possibilities Dialogue Series: Volume 2 Dialogues*
10. *Prison Possibilities Dialogue Series: Volume 3 Dialogues*
11. *Prison Possibilities Dialogue Series: Volume 4 Dialogues*
12. *Prison Possibilities Dialogue Series: Volume 5 Dialogues*
13. *Prison Possibilities Voluntary Exile: Concept*
14. *Prison Possibilities Correction Coaches: Concept*
15. *Prison Possibilities for Mexicans: Is A Boat Better than A Wall?*
16. *Prison Possibilities Family Time: A Reason to Thrive!*
17. *Prison Genius Pool: "So Much Genius In Jail."*
18. *Prison Possibilities Access Systems: Prisoner Access by Request*
19. *Prisoner's Lawyers Can Save The American Economy: Make A Buck Doing It & Be Thanked!*

20. Prisoner Family Talks, Days, Stays & Vacations: Connecting Helps Healing
21. Prisoner Writing Projects: Write To Heal, Start Over & Reconnect
22. Prison Cell Clearing & Blessing: Clear Entities, Chase Ghosts, and & Create Sacred Space
23. Prisoner Professors: Show You Are Aware Create Change With Care
24. Prison Reiki? Maybe Someday? A Gateway To Help Heal Prisons & America?
25. Judges and An Angel Rule On Possibilities: We Can Cut Sentences & Prison Costs
26. Ideas For Prison Wardens: Leadership Is Not Easy
27. Solitary Community: Could Community Support Cut Costs and Issues?
28. Prisoner Projects Communication Teams: Communications Can Change Lives
29. Motivating & Empowering Prisoners? Invite Prisoners To Find Their Motivation & Their Future
30. Prison Segmentation for Safety, Sanity, Security, Peace &
31. Prison Segmentationf for: Security

This book continues to carry the potential for rethinking that can help to reduce incarceration to those who we need to have there.

I want to trigger mindset shifts in the prisoners as well as employees and the community. We need a lot more Objective Productive Dialogues about Enhancing the lives of Prison Employees, Prisoners, Taxpayers and the Families of Each of these groups.

As I have been writing my books on Prisons, the complexity of the process has amazed me. I have some ideas of ways that might help, but I surrender to guidance.

My guidance suggests that we need a lot of creativity. Open minds on both sides of every issue can make great strides.

Open-mindedness is a real key point as closed minds may be one of the leading causes of the negativity that exists. Consider any argument that you ever had and remember that accommodation will usually follow a gesture of respect.

My perspective has been hard to achieve, but there seem to be some more dialogues that I would like to share:

1. Understanding the costs of Prisons is complicated, and states and programs have so many variables that most folks will be lost as I have been.

2. The humanity is difficult to balance because just like prison costs are difficult to measure, so are the human factors.

3. Change is needed to create balance and accountability so that fiscal responsibility is comparable between states, regions, and facilities.

4. The negative influence of trendy cultural shifts is not helping to achieve reasonable options.

5. Answers will not be simple or quick.

6. Creativity will be key to balance.

7. Those who care could share and communicate.

8. Uninvolved citizens do not help,

9. Voters have the power to change everything by their choices.

10. The answers will not come from someone who does not care so if you care then you just might want to get active in the American Political System.

2 - The Intensity of Space Density
{From - Prison Segmentation For Safety:}

The Intensity Of Density Can Cause Enormous Stress

3 - Space Segmentation
{From - Prison Segmentation For Safety}

Space Segmentation Could Decrease Density And Increase Security

4 - Space & Security Reactivity

The ideas that I put forth may have little to offer the residents and staff members at your particular location as all facilities are different. I am hopeful that many prisoners and prison staffers will benefit, so that is why I am writing.

The stories and pictures of incarceration that are seen on the outside may be inaccurate, and it may be that some facilities have reasonable space for all residents and staff members. I hope space is there for you or those you love.

Like so many activities there seem to be one major way of thinking and that may be how organizations set up in what seems like a logical flow. I do not think there is only one way that can make sense.

I believe that given the freedom to share without preemptive judgment could allow for ideas that may seem untraditional and inconceivable to become active. I think that all innovative thinking would fall into that category and create new possibilities for all sides of every issue.

Christopher Columbus epitomized my view quite well. All of us in American have benefitted from his inventiveness.

If you have adequate room in your facility, then you need not read much further. If on the other hand, congestion of activities and people are bothersome then I invite you to continue reading.

It is normal for human beings to require a certain amount of private space which will vary with each person. Some people like being close together in some situations.

I would not think that prison is a situation where people generally would like to be close. Oddly, there seems to be a level of emotional distance which happens naturally as a result of the dense use of space.

This can create emotional disconnects from normal behavior outside the walls. Emotional disconnects of any kind may generate complicating reactiveness which may remain dormant for a time.

I ponder the complexity of that pattern and wonder whether future explosive consequences may happen unexpectedly. Recent events seem to support my concerns.

5 - Space Can Help Reduce Stress
{From - Prison Segmentation For Safety}

Prisoners can be influenced by the space available to them. Space Density can be stifling while spaciousness can promote creativity and peaceful co-existence.

True as that statement is, there is a limit to the space available. The point that I would raise again, already, still is the need for creativity and thinking outside the box about the allocation and use of the space available with a frugal prevailing perspective as it is unlikely that change will come quickly without it.

There can be a reality of creative thought that can change utility and increase benefit. The stakes are high in prison, for the prisons, the prisoners, the prison staff's families, the prisoner's families, the taxpayer and their families, the government agencies, the states and municipalities, the national government and our society as a whole.

We can change the system, and we will but the big question is – "How many lives will be un-optimized by any chaos that exists until we start the necessary changes?" We are all in the boat, and it is sinking.

I can almost hear the voices saying that the problem does not affect me and my answer to that is BSSS (Bull Stinky Solid Stuff).

All taxpayers are affected by the costs of prisons. All citizens are worthy of as much freedom as their behavior allows.

6 - How Can Space Be Used Differently?
{From - Prison Segmentation For Safety}

Earlier I wrote a Prison book titled *Prison Possibilities Access Systems: Prisoner Access by Request.* That book started a discussion about access to space and how prisoners can flow through that space.

I would encourage many conversations about Safety, Sanity, Security, Peace & Space use. The objective of the conversations would be about how to use space more wisely.

If we begin to think of prisons as a 24-hour facility, we can then believe that certain areas could be progressively developed to be better utilized. Hospitals and Airports have many functions going on around the clock, and these different shifts rarely get in the way of each other.

With the right motivations and access controls, we could begin to the progressive refit of our facilities to be much safer, much more secure, much more prisoner-friendly, much more prison staff friendly, much less stressful and much more peaceful.

We could coincidentally reduce prison conflicts, increase correction officers safety, reduce medical costs incidental to conflicts, reduce lost corrections officer's time caused by being hurt scuffling with prisoners.

7 - Initial Analysis

Early on at no expense, we can begin to look at the occupancy times for sections of the facility.

We need to know based on the programs in place, the total utilization of the primary function areas of the facility.

Next, we need to know all incidental times that prisoners who perform services are using those primary function areas to prepare for the major services that they provide.

Next, we need to know All the Primary Function areas that have blocks of time that are unavailable for prisoner access.

Next, we need to know the lesser used areas of the prison and all the blocks of time that those areas are empty of prisoners and how long those blocks of time are.

Next, we will need to know all the times when the cell blocks that prisoners sleep in are empty and not accessible to the prisoners.

Next, we need to look at the service areas and find all the service area space that is empty for periods of time and how long those periods are and what options might be possible for all that open space if there were new occupancy plans.

This review needs to be 24 hours broad to begin to show real possibilities.

8 - Space Use Security Goals

Facilities can endeavor to create a B shift and a C Shift that will offer great new freedom possibilities for prisoners. Being able to select patterns or tracks of new segmentation that carries opportunities will promote feelings of personal empowerment and peace.

The lessening of feelings of overcrowding within the facility may reduce risks for staff and prisoners alike.

Many stories share some unplanned segmentation of groups of inmates where they have grouped themselves based on ethnic or cultural orientations or other common interest orientations. The concept shared here is not organized to work against those choices of alignment by prisoner's interests but to increase freedom and space.

This concept should prove helpful to all prisoners and staff by spreading out the residents and allowing more space per prisoner at many times.

Each facility that chooses to make some adjustments based on this idea could receive security benefits by having residents spread throughout the facility around the clock.

Management that chooses to make some adjustments based on this idea could have stress reduction throughout, and prisoners who are at higher risk may be more easily separated from potential conflicts with others.

9 - Essential Service In the Segments
{From - Prison Segmentation For Safety}

Planning will be needed to provide all required benefits to all prisoners, and that will have to be planned before any changes.

While space use is important, so are the full range of rights and privileges for each prisoner.

Of course, prisoners could be returned to the general population whenever necessary for prison operations.

The hope with this system would be the benefit of additional space and freedom which could ultimately be instrumental in making a case for more creative changes to the institutional control systems within the system.

The simplest way to move forward can be the teamwork that seems lacking in prison. Ideally, we can move towards a scenario where the underprivileged of yesterday can begin to become the insurers of privileges for those who without their efforts would be doomed to the injustices of the past.

Teamwork and justice and freedom while the goals of the Formation of this country may have been lost to many. Let us now use the devastation of incarceration to identify and change the problems of yesteryear and create a new bounty of possibilities now. Let us all seek peace as we build on the foundation of freedom that has nurtured our predecessors in the country that we treasure.

10 - How Would Security Segmentation Work?

The idea is to provide opportunities to spread people out and improve possibilities for all. For most of the residents (probably 90%), things could stay pretty similar for awhile unless someone wanted to step up and out on a path of making things better for everybody. You ought to volunteer.

Most buildings have a natural degree of segmentation based on structural design and function of sections. It is quite common to have busy areas in most buildings throughout the day that is crowded during certain times and empty during others.

At Noon each day, many dining areas will be crowded while an hour before or after may have substantially different visitors. Breakfast time and dinner time will be similar.

Hospital with three schedules will have many more variations where Day shift is busiest, but there are also B shift visitors and C shift guests in the dining areas at all kinds of hours around the clock or in designated time blocks around the clock.

Prisons who rely on one shift for everything on a fixed, inflexible schedule may think they are reasonable and proper. While they may well be correct, I suggest that creative thought can reduce stress and be more user-friendly for all the residents, staff and visitors.

Prisons who increase their shifting could find their density in all areas different, and that could be advantageous during a time of upheaval.

11 - Segmentation Could Decrease Density

On the title page, you see there are three different sized sections which are different sizes than the image that I used on the cover.

Consider the cover image as representative of a prison which has no shift segments and everybody is in the standard segmentation of the facility.

Now consider the title page as if the larger image is 90 percent of the image of the cover page. The next smaller image on the title page represents the first segmentation effort which could be up to 5% of the cover page.

The next smaller image on the title page represents the second segmentation effort which could be up to 5% of the image of the cover page.

In this little visual, I hope that you see that there has been little change but many options created for the softening of the comfort level for all.

The options created could be potential game changers for the ones who have the opportunity to separate themselves from the chaos of the larger crowd. Being freer to settle down alone may be enough to justify the effort.

Prisons could gain a lot be choosing to enhance creativity through segmentation.

12 - Segmentation Can Be Foundational

Segmentation can provide a separation between the shifts and many people who are less than compatible. The added safety zones can allow for fewer complications from the stressful sharing of space with others.

Many could have a new peace experience which may nurture all kinds of creativity. Perhaps even a kind of respite from the prison norm.

Peaceful time separating them from their normal patterns could allow their mind to settle down and find some privacy, peace, and sanity.

Citizens in much less stressful situations need a break or mental health day. Prisoners also could benefit from separation from the day to day grind.

I wrote an earlier book about what I termed Corrections Coaches which might be a career development path for officers someday. Segmentation paired with coaching could evolve as a privilege that disciplined residents could benefit from when their behavior was peaceful and cooperative.

Once there is an evolution of thinking, there could be a flood of proposals coming up to the administration.

13 - Space Reorganizational Ideas

Incremental implementation would be the most feasible plan as justifying expense does not have a predetermined path.

Planning and progressive development would be required to set this up, but I think over time that the payback would be extremely beneficial.

It may be most helpful to encourage prisoner suggestions as discussed in Prison Possibilities Dialogue Series and the earlier Segmentation Book about safety. Just one page per idea and the most likely ideas to consider will be ones that:

1. Follow the Dialogue rules and are focused on the whole community being benefitted and not any particular person.

2. Design Criteria to Request
   a. A simple 200-word article about an idea that has the capability to be the seed of a positive perspective shift for the readers of it.
   b. No venting or blaming
   c. Messages that could help heal, release, seed, process, understand, rethink, conceptualize, organize and otherwise analyze the who, what, when, where, how and why of an event.
   d. Understanding things can allow new perspectives of the ways that everything and everyone fit into the grand scheme of things.
   e. Life is an experience, and it has a timeline for us all.

    f. "The desired format is a single Page Configuration >200 words <220 Words, in a 6 x 9 book format with all .5 margins, Title Font 20 Pt. Times New Roman, Body Font 14 Pt. Times New Roman. Adherence to the desired format will go a long way to simplify the process for me. Thank You."

3. Evaluation teams to develop the ideas for prisoners to recommend.

4. Evaluation teams to develop the ideas for prison staffers to recommend.

14 - Redesign Teams

While dialogues of potential programs will help to start the segmentation process, the next step is the design of criteria for the application that was written about.

The obstacle will be that this is not likely to be embraced as a breakthrough process that will save volumes of money and the design concepts will need to be well developed before any changes are proposed.

The success of the whole program may depend on the early efforts so there should be no rush to do "something" as that may be a huge mistake. Initially, I would suggest that the team choose a single night of segmentation for a single person so that the whole experience can be studied in detail.

The prisoners and prison staff will have their own perspectives on how to do the process, but for me some key components to be considered are:

- An emphasis on there being no start-up monies expected from the facility except money that would need to be spent routinely that is well documented so there can be no misunderstanding later that the funds may seem to be misused.

- An emphasis on there being no promises made or expected to be made to, or for or by participants. Everybody would support best by starting with the idea of experiencing an effort that COULD SOMEDAY lead to a welcome change in the system.

- An emphasis on there being multiple potential paths for people of various interests and an interest in spreading out to align and serve as many individuals who demonstrate integrity and willingness to work hard towards getting out and staying out.

- An emphasis on taking each and every complaint seriously, so that integrity of balance and fairness is evident.

- Each complaint should be investigated, documented, answered and shared with administration.

- Each new complaint could automatically pause the processing of new proposals.

- Submissions received after a complaint should be accumulated, receipt dated and timed, acknowledged and queued for later consideration.

- Besides prep for release, proposals for prison experience enhancement should be evaluated.

- Benefits distributed in three categories would show real progress:

    1. Prisoner's benefit
    2. Prison Staff benefit
    3. Taxpayer's benefit

15 - Future Prison Segment Sizes - Whichever Works Best

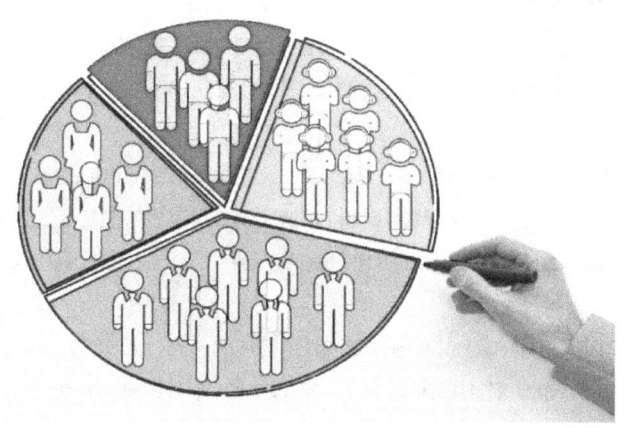

16 - Rehabilitation
{From - Prison Segmentation For Safety}

A goal that some folks expect of incarceration is rehabilitation. I hear little about successes in that pursuit but would be delighted to hear of new potentials for that to happen.

I believe that success is more likely if there can be more open-minded, creative thought applied to everything related to prisons and jails and other parts of the legal system.

There seem to be opposing positions on each side of every issue, and I feel that tendency on both the side of administration and the side that is sensitive to the incarcerated. I suggest to both points of view that there is needed a side to all things that minimize opposition and promote team efforts to finesse new ideas that benefit all the interested parties which would include the Prisons, the Prisoners and especially the taxpayers.

All three interests are diminished by opposition by anybody to anything. Interestingly, I see greater value in saying and doing nothing than there is in opposing anything suggested by anybody.

Fractional progress can b much more efficient than absolute objection. If all parties agree on the part of an idea, then we have real progress.

With any luck in prison, Congress may adopt the process and America can thrive. Prisons and Prisoners and taxpayers can lead the way. My question is – Will You? Will We? Will They?

17 - Universal Prayer For Prisons

Prayer Suggestion For Prisoners, Prison Staffers, Public Officials, Medical Practitioners, and Correction Officers/Coaches

God Almighty

I/We recognize you as the source of all good, all healing, all wholeness, all wellness and all support for your offspring in all matters.

I/We unify with your Divine Will and strive to respect all your children in all situations with the same dignity and respect that you do. We appreciate your helpful direction, guidance, and protection as we go out to interact with all your children in the world.

I/We claim our highest skilled functional awareness under your direction and our ability to hear the things to do and the words to say. I/We claim all the healing needed for all of us is now optimized as this claim is declared. As we invite all this or better now, we also ask for you to have us do nothing if that is the best for all.

I/We accept that the optimized situation for all is started, increased and fulfilled now.

I/we offer my/our sincere Thanks to you Dear God, AND SO IT IS!

18 - Thank You

For
Considering
These
Ideas

19 - Don't Worry Ever

Ever

It Does Not Help Prayer Still Does!

Resource: http://www.Create-A-Prayer.com

20 - Resource Books

Distant Healing Sessions (or Join Mail List) – Write To mikewann@voicenet.com

Books by Rev. Mike at **www.Amazon.com**

Veterans Healing Six Pack
1. *Trauma Healing Options for VA Hospitals: Help for Veterans to Own Their Healing and their future.*
2. *Trauma Healing Action Steps for Veterans: Help to Start Healing*
3. *Trauma Healing Action Steps for Veterans: Empowerment*
4. *Trauma Healing Action Steps for Veterans: Forgiveness*
5. *Trauma Healing Action Steps for Veterans: Thought Freedom*
6. *Tea For Veterans: Welcome One Home*

PTSD Power Pack:
1. *The PTSD Project: Turn Pain To Power*
2. *PTSD & Soul Retrieval: Putting One Back Together*
3. *PTSD & The Purple PAD: Calling all Scientists and PTSD Patients*

Angel Raphael Speaks Volume 1: Take Courage! God Has Healing in Store for You!
Angel Raphael Speaks Volume 2: Take Courage! God Has Healing in Store for You!
Angel Raphael Speaks Volume 3: Take Courage! God Has Healing in Store for You!
Angel Raphael Speaks Volume 4: Angels, Addicts, Alcoholics & Prisoners – Oh Yeah!
Angel Raphael Speaks Volume 5: Prisoners Caring for Alcoholics - Australia In Miniature Projects Intro
Angel Raphael Speaks Volume 6: Prisoners Caring for Addicts - Australia In Miniature For Addicts
Reiki Journaling from Japan
Reiki Is Alive: God's Great Gift
Four Parts to Healing
Distant Healing: We Are All Connected
Stress Release Energy Work: How To Cope
Does Reiki Love Heal Cancer?
Group Consciousness
Salute To Philadelphia VA Medical Center: Thank You
Reiki Transcript for Reiki 2 & 3 Channels: Dr. Usui Is That You?
God Bless Kindle & Amazon
Puppies Are Different From People
If Your Dog Dies
Toy Guns Are Obsolete

Great Spirit Made Children With Red Skin: AND
The Cage of Fear: Is Not Locked
God Made Children Red, Yellow, Brown, Black & White: Greet Each Child With Kindness
Emergency Medical Kindness In The Cradle Of Liberty: Big City - Cracked Bell
Angels Are Always Around Addicts and Addicts: Help Is Near Now! Invite It In!
Angels Are Always Around Addicts and Alcoholics: Volume 2 - Tools To Help Re-Light Your Life
Prison Jobs Now: Providing Care For Addicts And Addicts
Controlled Care Communities Concept
Prison Possibilities Dialogue Series: Concept
Prison Possibilities Dialogue Series: Volume 2, 3, 4, 5 Dialogues
Prison Possibilities Voluntary Exile
Prison Possibilities Corrections Coaches
Prison Possibilities For Mexicans: Is A Boat Better Than A Wall?
Prison Possibilities Family Time: A Reason to Thrive!
Prison Genius Pool: "So Much Genius In Jail."
Prison Possibilities Access Control: Prisoner Access by Request
Prisoner's Lawyers Can Save The American Economy: Make A Buck Doing It & Be Thanked!
Prisoner Family Talks, Days, Stays & Vacations: Connecting Helps Healing
Prisoner Writing Projects: Write To Heal, Start Over & Reconnect
Prison Cell Clearing & Blessing: Clear Entities, Chase Ghosts, and & Create Sacred Space
Prisoner Professors: Show You Are Aware Create Change With Care
Prison Reiki? Maybe Someday? A Gateway To Help Heal Prisons & America?
Judges and An Angel Rule On Possibilities: We Can Cut Sentences & Prison Costs
Ideas For Prison Wardens: Leadership Is Not Easy
Solitary Community: Could Community Support Cut Costs and Issues?
Prison Project Communications Team: Communications Can Change Lives
Motivating & Empowering Prisoners? Invite Prisoners To Find Their Motivation
Prison Segmentation For Safety, And Sanity, Security, Peace and Space
Prison Segmentation For Security
Dowsing for Prisoners; Answers from Above

Little Books at Kindle.com by Rev. Mike:
English Medical History Questionnaire For Non-English Speakers
English Language Helper For Non-English Speakers
Wise Wonderful Women Are The Well Of The Family
Answers for Test & Research: Dowsing Power
Crisis? Reiki! Baby? Reiki!
Bible References For Healing
Angel Raphael Speaks – Prisons
Angel Raphael Speaks – Veterans
The Saint Off Interstate 95

21 - Angels Please Prayers

Addict's

Angels of Healing Selected
Help Me to Stay Directed
Come To Me From The Sky
I Am Ready to Succeed Not Try
If I Don't Invite You In
I Might Not Win
I Have Been Lost For Too Long
Help Me To Stay Strong

Alcoholic's

Angels of Healing On High
Help Me to Stay Dry
Come To Me From The Sky
I Am Ready to Succeed Not Try
If I Don't Invite You In
I Might Not Win
I Have Been Lost For Too Long
Help Me To Stay Strong

From

http://AngelRaphaelSpeaks.com/AAAAAAA/

22 - Private Channeling

Angel Raphael Speaks a series of free messages that are channeled through Reverend Mike Wanner for the Highest good and Highest Healing of all concerned.

Many questions arise about Reverend Mike doing private channeling, and he does help with that so e-mail him.

Reverend Mike is available worldwide as a psychic channel, emotional release facilitator, spiritual energy practitioner & teacher, and public speaker. He looks forward to meeting you soon!

Email - mikewann@voicenet.com 215-342-1270 PRIVATE SPIRITUAL READINGS/channelings or Spiritual Healing Sessions: Telephone or in person. Rev. Mike is available for private, one-on-one intuitive sessions with you, his Guide Family, and your Guides. He helps by offering clarity on emotional situations about your life, your purpose, your spirituality, and the release of stuffed emotions and cellular memory.
Connect to the love of your Guides today!
Contact Rev. Mike for an appointment.
Sessions available:
- Spiritual Readings
- Angel Channeling
- Distant Reiki Healing
- Remote Clearing of Stuffed Emotions
- Distant Clearing Cellular Memory
- Distant Clearing Energy Blockages
- Remote Clearing of the Chakras
- Customized needs
- Mastermind dowsing responses to yes/no direction finding questions.

Rev. Mike is a facilitator of healing. He brings you and the Divine together so that you can align with the Divine and have a great time and a great life. All healing is between you and God, as it should be. Go ahead and start without Rev. Mike. Visit his prayer site http://www.Create-A-Prayer.com. Take the first step NOW.

23 - Reverend Mike Wanner

Rev. Mike Wanner started his Metaphysical and Ministerial studies with Reiki in 1993 and had studied seven styles of Reiki in the U.S., Japan, Canada, Denmark and Australia. He is certified to teach. He became certified to teach Integrated Energy Therapy in 1999 and co-taught the first IET class of the new Millennium. Mike began dowsing in 2001.

Ordained as a Metaphysical Minister of the International Metaphysical Ministry and an Interfaith Minister of the Circle of Miracles Ministry, Rev. Mike practices and teaches spiritual energy therapies in the Philadelphia Area.

Rev. Mike holds ministerial degrees from the University of Metaphysics and the University of Sedona. He is a Pastoral Care Associate of Aria - Frankford Hospital. He taught at the National Academy of Massage Therapy and Health Sciences.

Rev. Mike was a faculty member of the Medical Mission Sister's Center for Human Integration's School of Integrated Body/Mind Therapies in Fox Chase, Philadelphia, PA for twelve years.

Rev. Mike is licensed by the teaching of Intuitional Metaphysics to practice Spiritual Healing and Scientific Prayer. Mike is also a Prayer therapist.

Rev. Mike was elected in 2007 to the status of "Fellow of the American Institute of Stress."

In 2008, Rev. Mike became a practitioner of Coincidental Recognition as he incorporated the CoRe System into his spiritual healing practice.

In 2009, Rev. Mike trademarked a new healing process called Quantum Quatro! Subtle Energy System Support®.

In 2011, Rev. Mike joined the outreach program known as the Health Advantage Group.

In 2012, Rev. Mike became a Certified Professional Coach by The Master Coaching Academy and Joined the Personal Empowerment Group.

Before his Metaphysical, Ministerial and Coaching studies, Rev. Mike worked for Sears Roebuck and Co. while in High School and after graduation, until he joined the U. S. Air Force in 1965. He returned to Sears from Vietnam in 1969 and stayed until 1978. His final Sears assignment was as an efficiency expert in Methods - Operational Research and Development.

He volunteered with Burholme Emergency Medical Services from 1969 and is still a Life Member and Board of Directors Member. He started a private ambulance company in 1975 and worked professionally in the field until 2001 when he devoted his full attention to real estate investing, healing, coaching, and writing.

www.ingramcontent.com/pod-product-compliance
Lightning Source LLC
Chambersburg PA
CBHW050034230526
45470CB00003B/1275